44 Secrets for Great Soccer Dribbling Skills

Mirsad Hasic

Copyright © Mirsad Hasic

All rights reserved.

ISBN: 1492390828
ISBN-13: 978-1492390824

DEDICATION

I dedicate this book all soccer players around the world.

CONTENTS

	Acknowledgments	i
1	Dribbling in Wrong Situations	1
2	Keeping Yourself Relaxed	Pg 4
3	Playing Futsal	Pg 7
4	Confidence is Everything	Pg 9
5	Finding Weaknesses	Pg 12
6	Being too Nervous	Pg 14
7	Dare to Fail	Pg 16
8	Disguising Your Intention	Pg 18
9	Vary Your Moves	Pg 20
10	Incomplete Moves	Pg 22
11	Skip The Fancy Moves	Pg 24
12	Keep Your Look Up	Pg 26
13	Being Innovative	Pg 28
14	Combo Moves	Pg 30
15	Using all Parts of Your Foot	Pg 32
16	Focus on Using Your Arms	Pg 34

17	Changing Your Pace Gear	Pg 36
18	How Many is Enough	Pg 38
19	Performing The Move Too Early	Pg 40
20	Devote Some Time to Your Best Moves	Pg 42
21	Focus on The Second Touch	Pg 44
22	Beyond The Dribbling Duel Mode	Pg 46
23	Importance of Your Weak Leg	Pg 49
24	Importance of Strength	Pg 51
25	Set up Realistic Goals	Pg 53
26	Track Your Progress	Pg 56
27	Watch Professional Games	Pg 58
28	Ask Your Friends to Evaluate Your Moves	Pg 61
29	Using a Smaller Ball	Pg 63
30	Surprising Moment	Pg 65
31	Anticipate Like The Pros	Pg 67
32	Discovering Your Own Dribbling Style	Pg 69
33	Get The Ball Back	Pg 71
34	Right Moves at Right Time	Pg 73
35	Body Feints	Pg 75

36	Balance Foot	Pg 77
37	Dropping The Shoulder	Pg 79
38	Wait for The Opponent	Pg 81
39	Ignoring Provoking Opponents	Pg 83
40	Get Inspired by Your Teammates	Pg 85
41	Improving Your Hop	Pg 87
42	Visualizing Your Moves	Pg 89
43	Shielding The Ball	Pg 91
44	Touches on The Ball	Pg 93

ACKNOWLEDGMENTS

I would like to thank my family for their support.

1 DRIBBLING IN WRONG SITUATIONS

One of the biggest mistakes players make when trying to get past their opponents is to pick the wrong situations.

I don't know how many times I've seen players trying to get around a challenger when they have at least one better positioned teammate in place and ready to finish the attack.

Not only is this frustrating as a player, it also shows contempt against your teammates.

Why?

Because even though you are not saying it out loud, your way of playing speaks for itself: "I don't care about "the team". I just want to make myself look great."

I really need you to think about the way you play your game.

You will not win anything from chasing your own glory by trying to prove how good you are at dribbling.

Leaving the rest of your teammates to watch your solo performance is not what you might call a team effort.

I'm sure you already know that soccer is not a lone sport where you get to play for yourself against another.

There are 10 more players on the field, all of whom will be giving their all to win the game as a team.

So if you're looking for superstardom on the pitch at a cost to the squad, then soccer is perhaps not the right game for you.

Another common mistake many rookie players make is to dribble on their own side of the field.

A smart, experienced player will never risk losing the ball, and a potential goal, to an opponent by doing this.

Instead, he will pass the ball safely to an unmarked teammate who would then have the opportunity to get the ball moving over to the opponent's side of the pitch.

I know it can be tempting to show how skillful you are, but I promise you this: it's not worth it!

If you lose the ball by playing a selfish game, the whole team will blame you, especially if the rival side gets to score a goal because of it.

Too much "going it alone" and you run the risk of losing your place on the team in future games.

For example, trying to dribble during a counterattack, when the rest of your team is moving up the field, could result in your opponents scoring should you lose the ball to them.

I'm telling you this from my own personal experience.

I once made the mistake of trying to perform a nutmeg (playing the ball through the legs of an challenger) on an opponent just outside our 18 yard box.

However, this rival player was able to intercept my dribbling attempt and got himself a free scoring opportunity; one in which he successfully utilized.

We lost that game and I promised myself on that day that I'd never again dribble on my own side of the field, ever!

This was a perfect example of a selfish move. Instead of chasing my own glory, I should have picked a better alternative or just cleared the ball away.

However, my mistake cost us dearly as we lost the game because of my egotistical stance.

I should also say that my coach put me on the bench in the next game and told me I will sit there until I realize that soccer is a team sport and not a one man show!

So, always think about the consequences of your dribbling, and ask yourself if what you're about to do next is worth the consequences.

2 KEEPING YOURSELF RELAXED

Have you ever wondered how the greatest soccer players are able to perform their dribbling skills with such perfection, and maneuver past their opponents with seeming ease?

This is because those players are able to keep themselves composed, relaxed almost, thus allowing them to perform their dribbling skills faster, more accurately and with a higher degree of success.

We've all tried to dribble by an opponent while being completely rigid.

It's no easy task being cool, calm and collected in a game that pumps adrenaline and demands results, but composure of both body and mind is achievable, but like all skills, this is something that has to be learnt.

While it is easy to acknowledge in theory that you will play better when you can keep yourself calm, it is much harder to do in practice.

Although our brain is a truly amazing and advanced machine, it still needs programing if it's to behave how we need it to.

You can't simply imagine yourself in a relaxed state for it to happen.

No, you need to train the mind over time so that the way you think on the field becomes one of your natural behaviors.

I used to be really rigid on the soccer field and my dribbling attempts often ended in the ball bouncing off my feet in completely opposite directions to what I had planned.

I use to stumble a fair bit too, which made me look even more amateur.

It was really frustrating because during practice sessions I was totally relaxed, hyped up of course, but unperturbed nonetheless.

I could usually get past any teammate, but as soon as the game started I transformed into someone completely different and whole body became tense and inflexible.

So one day, I decided to take a different mental approach.

I promised myself that I would strive to stay focused on keeping myself more relaxed on the field no matter what!

As it happens, this became a real turning point for my game.

Suddenly I discovered that my dribbling skills began working on real opponents, just as they did during practice.

My teammates found this sudden transformation hard to believe. Jokingly, they would say they thought it was Lionel Messi dribbling though the opposition, not me.

This only helped to motivate me further, and in my head, I could almost hear the crowds applauding and cheering from the grandstand.

As my game lifted, the more I worked on staying focused and relaxed because I had truly discovered the benefits of doing so.

I can't give you a secret formula to being composed on the soccer field because there isn't one.

We might all be made of the same stuff, but none of us thinks and feels in the exact same way.

Therefore, you need to find your own relaxing point and start working on it during the games.

I also want to emphasize how easy it can be to fall into those same old habits even after you have developed a new mindset.

If you have been "hardwired" with rigidity, then this is natural to you, meaning it will always be there lurking in the subconscious mind waiting to return.

You can avoid this by becoming mindful!

Realize that if you want to become good at dribbling then you will need to start relaxing on the pitch and maintaining that technique.

A stiff player is never going to perform as well as he would do if he were more relaxed.

Drop your guard and you will surely start to reinforce those old bad habits you worked so hard to kick.

3 PLAYING FUTSAL

By improving your dribbling balance you will be a more flexible, quicker, and much more unpredictable player; one who is able to perform just that bit better than the others.

It's the little things that make the biggest difference, and improving balance will separate you from the rest of the team.

While you probably already know the importance of good balance when dribbling in soccer, you probably didn't know that this can be improved indirectly by playing futsal.

This small sided, hugely popular game, is played in high tempo all around the world. It is one of the main secrets as to why Brazilian players are some of the best on the planet when it comes to dribbling.

Pele, who is still seen by many as the best player who ever existed, said that without futsal he would never have gained such great dribbling balance, something he said, that was critical for his development as a world class player.

When playing futsal you are forced to focus on your dribbling technique.

As you get better at dribbling, you are indirectly improving your balance.

This is quite unavoidable due to the nature of the game.

However, you should not dribble on your own side of field.

As stated previously, if you lose the ball on your side of the pitch, then you are almost giving your opponents a free opportunity to score, or at least try to score, without too much pressure at all.

While futsal is usually played indoors, you don't necessarily have to find a hall as they can be pretty expensive to book, sometimes costing as much as $100 per hour depending on its condition and where in the world you live.

If the weather serves you well, you can find a street basketball field, set up small goals, and voila, you have your own futsal field in a jiff.

You will get most out of the game when you can find enough people to make up two teams equal in numbers.

Having two full sides will allow you to get a lot of dribbling opportunities in, and the more you dribble, the more you get to indirectly improve your balance.

Back in the day, we used to play futsal whenever we got the chance.

Not only was I able to improve my dribbling balance, but I was also able to further develop my overall ball skills too.

These things combined gave me a huge advantage for when I began to play later on in more serious matches.

So there you have it.

It's now your responsibility to take advantage of this newfound knowledge and use it to take your dribbling skills up to the next level.

I guarantee that if you play competitive games of futsal at least once per week, then you will, without doubt, notice an improvement in your balance as you challenge your opponents in dribbling duels.

4 CONFIDENCE IS EVERYTHING

Have you ever heard the saying: If you don't believe in your goals, then you will never reach them?

Confidence in soccer is what separates you from the rest of the players.

Having self-assurance, or not as the case may be, is also something that separates the winners from losers.

Lacking confidence when trying to dribble your opponents is like trying to drive a car without wheels, meaning you will never get anywhere.

Poise on the field is one of the most critical ingredients for becoming a master at dribbling.

So if you're serious about upping your game, then you really do need to start paying attention to this.

When I first started out playing soccer, I was probably the worst dribbler on our team.

Seriously, I couldn't even maneuver around our coach and this guy was almost 60 years old and quite overweight!

My one remaining problem was that I still lacked confidence to perform my newly acquired skills when I needed them the most.

In other words, I was still unable to dribble past my coach when there was pressure to do so, even though most of the other players could do this blindfolded.

One day I was watching our first team practice and there was this player from Brazil who was exceptionally good at dribbling.

It seemed impossible for anyone to take the ball from him once he got it.

You could just seem how frustrated the other players were by their inability to stop him.

I remember thinking how I wished I could be at least half good as he was.

After the practice I approached him and asked how I could become better at dribbling.

He gave me some practical tips but made a point to place an emphasis on self-confidence.

He said, and I quote: "If you don't have confidence in your ability then you will never be able to dribble around your opponents.

You see, in your own mind you have already made the conclusion, albeit a subconscious one, that it will not be possible.

On the next game I decided to take his advice onboard and try this approach.

I told myself repeatedly that today I will play with confidence and nothing else matters!

This was a real eye opener and I never expected the results I got.

I was able to dribble around most of my opponents without any problems at all, and for every dribbling raid, my confidence was pushed that bit further in the positive direction.

Building confidence will have a huge impact on your dribbling success, but without it you will really struggle getting past your opponents on the pitch.

Too many failed attempts and you will inevitably become disheartened and eventually find no pleasure in competitive soccer.

Make sure you remember that statement in your next game: "Building confidence will have a HUGE impact on your dribbling success."

Implement what I've discussed in this section, and you WILL improve your game – guaranteed!

5 FINDING WEAKNESSES

In order to get past your opponent you will need to identify his weaknesses (we each have our own no matter how good we might be).

This will typically include things like whether he is slow, late into the situation, or has poor tackling skills, etc.

Whatever the case, you should try to identify these weaknesses and turn them against him.

If you do this well, you will have a huge advantage over your opponent from the outset.

In my experience, the most obvious weakness is the non-kicking leg of an opponent.

By going in the direction of his weak leg you will be able to get past most of your opponents, that is, providing you perform the move with accuracy.

This works even better against slower players.

Here, the trick is to perform your moves quickly and with confident determination.

It's true that you can quite often win simply by being a fast player with good ball control skills.

However, this is not always enough.

As you face more skillful opponents, then you will start to see the importance of emphasizing their weaknesses in order to get the better of them.

When I was 20 years old, I remember how we were playing a national cup game and facing a first division club with some really great players.

I mean, these are the ones you see on TV, and suddenly, there I was, preparing to play against them.

I still recall how I needed to pinch myself to realize this was really happening and not just a dream.

During that game, I was playing at the flank and facing an incredibly skillful defender, maybe the best one they had.

I can remember how anxious I became as every single attempt to get past him failed miserably.

My strategy needed to be refined, and pronto. I studied him for a few minutes during the game to try and identify where his weaknesses might lie.

I soon noticed how he was having problems with moving to the left.

I also noticed how he compensated by implementing a well thought out routine and obvious understanding of the game.

During a counter attack I found myself in a one on one challenge against him.

I decided to make him believe I would go to the right (which I did in the previous dribbling attempts), but when the time was right I maneuvered to the left instead.

I decided that a step over would be the ideal move to perform and it worked a treat!

I got past him, and then passed the ball to a teammate who was free in the 18 yard box, and we scored. Now that's teamwork!

We lost the game, as we expected to, with the final result at 8-1. But I will always remember this particular situation, and this is just one example of how you can turn an opponent's weakness to your own advantage.

6 BEING TOO NERVOUS

There is nothing wrong with being a little nervous when trying to dribble your opponents.

In fact, it's completely natural and helps to keep you on your toes, so to speak.

However, nervousness should not reach a point where you are so jumpy that you can't even perform the moves you need to do.

I've seen players performing amazing moves during the practice, but during the actual game these same players stumbled on the ball and couldn't even get the most basic maneuvers right.

When a player is too nervous on the pitch, both his mind and his body becomes out of sync, and that obviously has a negative impact on his dribbling performance.

This was something I struggled with myself until I recognized it and made some adjustments to my mindset.

So if you can identify with any of the above, at least you know there's a solution if you choose to work at it.

For me, I got to the point where I started to enjoy soccer practice more than the actual games.

This was simply because I could perform much better in practice sessions than I could in the real matches, but I wasn't happy about that at all.

This was something which continued to frustrate me for a while until the day came where I made a conscious decision to seriously do something about my nervousness on the field.

One thing I did was to carefully study great soccer dribblers like Ronaldinho and Messi.

Observing the way they performed their dribbling skills actually taught me a great deal

I spent at least one hour before every game watching these fine players and imaging that I was one of them.

Now this might sound a little like fantasy, or wishful thinking, but believe me when I say this really did help to better prepare me a during the games that followed.

Another strategy is to have someone record your games and then cut and paste your best moves into a single clip.

Once you have your edited film, simply watch and analyze your performance over and over until you know what you did and why it worked in the given situation.

Trust me. Scrutinizing your game is something that really does work when you take it seriously.

It might sound a bit brash, but oftentimes I could barely believe the guy in the clips performing these awesome moves and dribbling around his opponents was actually me!

By watching these "Best of Me" clips I was able to realize that if I have done it once then surely I could do it again. All I had to do was work at it until such playing became natural to the way I performed during matches. The key here is to get your focus in the right direction and stay focused.

So, if you are one of those players who find himself really nervous when trying to dribble during games, then I recommend you try my approach. Take it seriously and I can guarantee that you WILL improve!

7 DARE TO FAIL

You will not become a dribbling wizard after one session, one week or even one month.

No, it takes some time and a lot of dedicated effort before reaching the level where you are able to dribble a player faster and easier than tying your own shoelace, but it can be done.

All you have to do is want it enough.

Understand that you will fail a lot of the time as you strive to improve, but whatever you do never let this set you back and stop you from practicing.

Remember, there can be no success without some failure along the way.

We actually learn more about ourselves from our failures than our successes.

Failing is all part of the improvement game.

It's a mistake to assume your every dribbling attempt will be a success – no matter how good you become – because this is just not a realistic expectation.

You will always face different types of players in different situations, where some will be extremely skillful while others are less so.

What you must never do is to become complacent.

Again, failure is not on inevitable but it's good for you as it gives you an opportunity to learn from your mistakes and flip them into something better for those future games.

Failure to learn from your mistakes, however, will have a reverse effect.

Not only will you not improve, but you also run the risk of becoming worse over time, instead of better.

One of my greatest mistakes, as my dribbling improved, was to get a little too cocky. I would sometimes find myself trying to perform fancy maneuvers, something that the spectators would love.

In other words, I had become something of a showoff!

However, just because a move looks fancy and skillful that doesn't mean it is necessarily the most efficient one at the time.

This was something I soon began to realize, and the time had come to get real again.

I can remember during a cup semi-final once where we had a counter attack. The whole team was moving up the field and we were four players against only two opponents.

I was running with the ball and had three passing opportunities yet I chose to try a nutmeg on the opponent but failed miserably.

My opponent regained control of the ball and successfully crossed it to his striker. The striker was completely unmarked which allowed him to just dribble our goalie and score with relative ease.

We lost the game with the final score at1-0. I still blame myself for that defeat to this day because I felt that I let down the entire team!

What you should learn from this is the fact that you should always carefully examine your options before trying to dribble an opponent.

Failure to way up the situation and make the right decision could literally lose you the match.

8 DISGUISING YOUR INTENTION

One of the best kept secrets to being a dribbling ace is to learn the art of disguising your intentions for as long as possible.

The longer you can mask your intent the more success you will have with your dribbling raids.

To give you a simple example, let's take a look at the step over move (also known as the pedalada, the Denílson, or the scissors) which is one of the most efficient skills for successfully getting past your opponent.

In this move you are stepping over the ball at one side in order to have the opponent move in that direction.

Immediately after your foot touches the ground, you then push the ball in the opposite direction.

So let's imagine that you are right footed and approaching an opponent.

You would step over the ball with the right leg while at the same time aligning your body to the right.

As the opponent moves his body to this side you then move the ball to the left and get past, while leaving him out of balance.

What you have done here is to disguise your intention.

If you were just stepping over the ball without moving your body to the right, your opponent would still be in balance and therefore have a much better chance of clearing the ball.

However, you had him believe that you would actually go to the right by moving your body along with your right leg, but you didn't, you exploded in the opposite direction.

It is really important to remember this when you are performing the move.

Again, the whole intention here is to have the opponent thinking you will be going in one direction just as you shoot off in the opposite one.

If your dribbling attempts are not working then it is probably because your intentions are too obvious and therefore easy to read.

If this is so, then you need to start working on fixing it without delay.

The best thing you can do is to buddy up with one of your teammates and practice this skill together.

Let him decide whether he finds your moves convincing or not.

If he immediately knows what your aims are then it's time to start working at masking your intentions.

Ask him to be brutally honest and not to hold back on his assessment.

After all, if he doesn't tell you the truth then you will never learn how to master the move correctly.

Failure to improve can only result in more underperformance on the pitch, and I'm certain that's not your intention!

9 VARY YOUR MOVES

Another of the common mistakes players make is to perform the same move on the same opponent over and over again, and that means they can read you like a book.

One general rule I have is to never perform the same move on the same opponent twice in a row.

I've noticed how repetition can become too predictable, meaning there's a much greater chance of a second attempt failing when it's the same move as the previous one.

Performing same or similar moves all the time might work just great on players who are not very experienced.

However, once you reach a higher level of gameplay you really do need to start upping your game and varying your dribbling attempts. Skillful players are quick to learn.

This means it doesn't take them long before they've memorized their opponents dribbling styles.

If you tend to stick with a single move then they will easily predict your intentions and stop your efforts without too much ado.

However, if you are one of those players who are totally unpredictable, then you will indirectly make your opponents more afraid of attacking.

This will obviously give you more advantage on the field.

In order to become a truly unpredictable player, you need to learn several different moves and master them completely.

Once mastered, you are able to perform well in low and high tempo games.

Varying your moves is critical if you are playing at the flank.

This is because you will be facing opponents in one V one dribbling duels all the time.

For example, let's say that you are playing as left midfielder and facing a really skillful and fast left fullback.

Now, if you are trying to go left all the time in order to serve a well-aimed cross to your strikers, the defender will quickly pick up on this and be able stop you in your tracks.

However, if you vary your moves by going to the right as well, then he will never be quite sure what you are up to next.

This will make him much more cautious and you much better able to out maneuver him.

As I mentioned before, this will give you an advantage on him and an opportunity to cross the ball without even needing to dribble.

The reason is simple. Because of your unpredictability, you will find that he gives you a lot more space because of his fear of being dribbled.

As you can see, varying your moves has a lot of advantages.

If you are not utilizing this strategy, then you are missing out on a great opportunity to dominate the game.

10 INCOMPLETE MOVES

In order to succeed with your dribbling raids you will need to master your soccer moves to such a level that you should be able to perform them in your sleep.

Incomplete moves will not get you anywhere because defenders will not be fooled by your dribbling attempts.

Remember, the whole purpose of a move is to make the opponent believe you will go one way while in reality you will shoot off in another direction.

It is better to master one single move rather than knowing ten incomplete moves that have little or no chance of ever getting you past a defender.

So, how do you figure out whether your moves are incomplete or not?

Well, as pointed out earlier in the book, a general rule of thumb is to practice all moves on your teammates first.

If you can't get past your mates during practice sessions, then it goes without saying that you will stand little chance of getting past any opponents during a real game.

I used to keep a notebook from where I monitored my dribbling attempts during the practice.

I then evaluated them afterwards to see if I could identify any areas that needed improvement.

What I did was to count the successful dribbling raids where I managed to dribble around one teammate and then do something useful with the ball afterwards.

If I was able to get past my teammates four times out of five, I then tried to analyze not only the unsuccessful attempt but also the successful ones.

We used to compare notes as a team, which was something else I found to be very beneficial.

Let's take a real example here.

There was one time during this analysis where I was looking at a step over.

What I discovered was that when I performed the step over I was not bending my knee enough.

This meant that my body didn't move to the side as much as it should do, and that made the move look unconvincing.

By correcting this one small thing meant I was then able to get past my teammates nine times out of ten.

Needless to say this boosted my self-confidence enough to successfully utilize the new improved move into games as well.

So you can see the importance now of identifying your incomplete moves.

Simply analyze what you are doing wrong and then look at how you can make the necessary improvements to better your skills.

I can assure you that once you realize the mistakes you're making and then work at correcting them, you will then have another great advantage to add in your dribbling arsenal!

Just remember that it's impossible to find a solution to a problem until first you know what the problem is.

11 SKIP THE FANCY MOVES

As a true soccer fanatic I agree that fancy moves are pure soccer candy and a joy for the eye to contemplate!

That said, I also believe that these moves are rarely efficient and belong more to a circus than a competitive soccer game.

Most coaches are not impressed with fancy footwork on the pitch.

In fact, some will get so wound up by it that they will put a player on the bench as a way of teaching him a lesson.

Fancy moves are nothing more than a collection of great soccer tricks, but they belong in backyard games where having fun is a number one priority.

It is much better to spend your valuable practice time working on dribbling moves that you can actually use in a game to get past your defender.

Working on becoming a performing clown will do nothing to enhance your game.

I've played with guys who could do truly amazing tricks with a soccer ball, but in most case their dribbling attempts were a complete failure.

This was because they focused too much time on fancy moves and too little time working on the skills that were needed on the field, where it matters most.

Fancy moves are not efficient enough to be used in high tempo games with skillful opponents.

Talented players are like hungry Rottweilers and they will not allow the competition a single moment to show off by entertaining the crowds with ball tricks.

Before learning a new move, I always categorize it first by asking myself the following question: is this a move I can use during a soccer game where the tempo is high?

If I decide that it's really a move that would be better suited in backyard soccer while having a kick-about with friends, then I won't waste time and energy trying to master it.

It is really important to be honest with yourself when categorizing moves in this way.

Failing to do so will cost you in a lot of wasted practice hours, time that you can spend working on far more important skills.

I have played with what many onlookers would consider great players simply because they were brilliant at fancy soccer moves.

However, the vast majority of these players were just average on the field.

This was because they never worked on moves that they could use in high tempo games against skillful opponents.

Those guys who can do fancy tricks with a soccer ball definitely have a talent for the game, yet they choose to use it to entertain rather than to compete.

So you need to ask yourself whether you want to be a successful dribbler and a real asset to your team, or, someone who entertains the crowd with circus moves before and after a match.

12 KEEP YOUR LOOK UP

When performing your move you need to keep an eye on both your opponent and the part of field behind him.

You can't just stare at the ball and focus directly on the move because you also need to know what is going on in front of you.

Failing to focus on the overall situation is one of the most common mistakes players make.

By focusing solely on the ball without knowing whether or not there are other opponents approaching is just a asking for defeat.

Even if you manage to keep control of the ball, there's still a very good chance that you will lose it as soon as you get past the first opponent.

By keeping your eyes buried on the ground directly in front of you is akin to playing blind.

I suggest you try another, more broad approach.

Get into the habit of keeping your head raised higher.

View your opponent at a 45 degree angle. This will roughly be the area of his navel.

With the head raised slightly higher it's still possible to keep an eye on the ball so that you don't stumble on it.

Furthermore, you are also able to keep an eye on what's going on around you, including the feet of your opponent.

This might sound like multitasking the impossible, especially if you are new to the world of soccer.

You're probably wondering how you're supposed to keep track on the ball, opponent, and the players around you, all at the same and yet still play a good game, right?

Don't worry.

This is nowhere near as difficult as it reads.

The sooner you start getting into the habit of looking up, the more natural it will become, and that means you will begin to play with more success on the soccer field.

As always, I recommend practicing with a buddy, maybe in your backyard to begin with.

Simply try to dribble around him by having your look focused at around 45 degrees.

Believe me, it won't take too long before you're doing this without even thinking about it.

Once you've gained a little confidence, try putting it into practice during your team training sessions.

And as with the practice of any new skills, don't be afraid to ask for feedback from the coach and your teammates.

Once you are able to successfully keep your look focused at around 45 degrees while maintaining good control on whatever move you are performing, then it's time to prepare for the final stage.

The last step is to put what you've learned into action during a real game and by trying it on real opponents.

Remember, if you can utilize it with success then keep it that way.

If you fail more often than not, rinse, repeat, and keep practicing until you become more competent!

13 BEING INNOVATIVE

A true dribbling wizard always has a secret move up his sleeve that he uses to surprise the opponent and leaves him wondering what just happened.

Such a move should be efficient and give you a real advantage on the field, while at the same time look impressive and cool.

It is hard to give you an exact formula on how to invent your own super move, but in general you should experiment a bit until you find something that works well for you personally.

When I invented my own move I got so good at it that I became the best player of the game.

Even the opponents were asking me after the match if I could teach them how to perform it.

During my junior years I was playing an international tournament in Germany.

A few weeks prior to it I had been working on a special move that I decided to try out during the tournament.

I was playing on the flank and as the game progressed, I realized that my defender was perhaps one of the best I had ever faced.

He was not only fast on his feet, but aggressive and able to tackle well too.

After failing to get past him during my dribbling attempts, I realized I needed to come up with something different, more unique, and so decided it was time for my special move.

I received the ball at the flank and approached the opponent at high speed while controlling the ball with the inside part of my foot.

Just as he was about a half yard from me, preparing his tackle, I pulled the ball with the sole and successfully curved it around him with the inside of my other foot.

He flew by me like a frustrated bull chasing a red flag.

This gave me a free path towards the goal where I was able to dribble past the defending goalie and score -1-0.

The game ended and we won that group game.

The funny thing was that several of the opponents approached me after the game and asked if I could teach them my special move, including the aggressive defender.

Being a good sportsman, I spent few minutes showing them how to do the move.

Alas, they just could not get it and they decided to give up.

This didn't surprise me because it took a lot of patience and persistence before I was able to perfect it.

This is why you should try to be innovative when learning different soccer moves, and come up with something that is unique to you.

Mastering your own special move(s) is a great way to completely confuse your opponents during a game.

14 COMBO MOVES

Have you ever watched a professional game on TV and seen players performing several moves in a row? I have, on numerous occasions, and usually left feeling amazed at how efficient these moves were when combined together?

The first time I saw a player performing a combo with great skill was during the 1998 World Cup.

It was Denilson (Brazil), and he made it look so effortless.

Yet in reality, I just knew it was something that must have taken great skill and time to master.

He performed ten step overs in a row, and at the end of the move the opponent was so confused that Denilson just slipped past his opponent without effort.

Another combo master was Zinedine Zidane.

This guy could makes it look as though he was performing the moves in slow motion, yet, his opponents were running around him in all directions like headless chickens, totally confused.

When done well, combos are great for confusing your opponent to the point where he won't be able to predict which direction you will head for.

Combos can also serve well as preparation for your final move.

By that, I mean you can use them to simply drive an opponent stir crazy, and then perform the final move to get past him.

There is no perfect formula for which type of moves you should combine.

This is something you need to discover for yourself, and find what best suits your skills.

For example, I like to perform 3-4 step-overs in a row before releasing my final move.

My final move could be anything from a fake kick to the Ronaldinho snake move, or 'Elastico'.

The best tip I can give to you is to experiment until you find your own unique style, and you will, and then once you do, try to implement it in the games to see if it's workable on the field.

It' probably best to try and limit yourself to a maximum of two moves per dribbling attempt.

After all, you want to get past your opponent as quickly as possible.

I've seen players performing 5-6 moves in a single combo.

Sometimes it works, but more often than not the time taken to perform these longer combos allows other opponents to catch up and regain possession of the ball.

So, to summarize it all up, try to perform maximum of two moves per combo, and keep practicing with different variations until you find your own unique style.

All that's left then is to work on refining your new moves until you can perform it/them with your eyes shut.

15 USING ALL PARTS OF YOUR FOOT

By using each part of your foot you will be able to dribble in all directions. This will obviously give you a huge advantage over your opponents.

I've seen a lot of players that tend to stick to the same move which involves using only a specific part of the foot.

By restricting themselves in this way they are limiting their options and ability to grow as a player.

Being able to dribble in different directions by using all parts of the foot really does help to develop your overall dribbling skills, so this is something that's definitely worth mastering.

Let's analyze three popular moves to illustrate the benefits of using all parts of the foot while dribbling.

The first one is the popular Puskas (a simple dribbling fake).

You can only perform this during low speed as it involves using the sole of the foot.

This is the ideal move to make when there are several opponents around you as you try to finish an attack with a quick and fast shot.

The second one is the step over which can be performed at both low and high speeds.

The step over involves using the outside part of the foot

This is an ideal move for getting past your opponent while playing at the flank, but it can also be highly efficient when you are at high speed and facing the opponent in the middle of the field.

The third one is performed by the Dutch wizard Cruyff.

It is achieved by pulling the ball backward with the inside part of your foot.

This move is ideal while faking a cross at the flank but it can also be used by fullbacks to get rid of aggressive strikers.

As you can see, using all parts of the foot when challenging your opponents is a crucial tactic for achieving real success on the soccer field.

If you want to be more than an average player, then I suggest that you pay close attention to my tips here and begin to implement them in your own game!

16 FOCUS ON USING YOUR ARMS

Your arms play a big role in the success of your dribbling attempts. You will use them to keep your balance, shield the ball, and also shake off unfair opponents.

Neglecting the important role that arms play is one of the biggest mistakes players new to the game can make.

Many aspiring soccer wannabes tend to focus completely on performing the move right, yet fail to reflect on how to involve the arms in their dribbling attempts.

Involving the arms is a part of dribbling that doesn't require a lot of time to master.

You just need to add it to your style of playing and work on using it until it becomes the norm.

To use your arms efficiently, just make sure they are involved in the motion, like when faking a shot, for example.

Here, you would not simply draw your leg back pretending that you are about to shoot, but also involve the arms as well.

In my experience, the most difficult thing with using the arms is actually remembering to involve them in your style of playing.

I have played games where I was able to use my arms really efficiently, but there were other times where I barely involved them in my dribbling at all, as pointed out by the coach.

The strategy I would recommend is that you start being mindful of using the arms during backyard soccer games with your friends.

Get into the habit of involving your arms and the habit will take over, meaning you will no longer have to think about it.

I must admit that in the beginning I was really poor at using my arms effectively when challenging opponents in dribbling duels.

It was only when my coach at the time spotted this that I was able to do something about it because I myself would never have noticed.

He explained that if I started to involve my arms when dribbling then I would see my success rate more than double.

I took his advice seriously and now my arms are a natural part of my play.

However, every once in a while do quickly check on myself, just to make sure I'm not falling back into old habits.

OK, so remember to involve your arms in your own style of dribbling.

If you're still unsure, get a coach or a more experienced team member to observe you and heed their feedback.

Get it right, and I can guarantee that you will be amazed at how much benefit you will get from using your arms effectively as you dribble.

17 CHANGING YOUR PACE GEAR

This is what separates the professionals from the amateurs.

Players who are able to slow their pace and then explode into a sudden run are the ones who have the most control.

Those who have not mastered 'pace' are much less effective at dribbling.

I see the art of dribbling as being two distinct parts.

Performing the actual move is one part and pace is the other.

Even if you can perform your move with bundled eyes, you will still not get too far until you master pace.

One of the greatest players and dribbling prodigies of all time, bar none, was the former Brazilian striker, Ronaldo.

His ability to change pace after performing the move was amazing to watch.

What really used to catch my attention was the way in which he would change pace the moment he got past the opponent.

He would simply switch into accelerate mode and leave the defeated one bewildered, wondering what had just happened!

Ronaldo's specialty was the step over move.

And when an opponent would turn around ready to pursue him after he'd passed, Ronaldo was usually long gone, already several yards in front and still gaining distance.

Just search for Ronaldo on YouTube and analyze his dribbling skills.

You will then see exactly what I mean by "changing the pace gear".

It matters little if you can dribble your opponent ten times in a row if he's able to easily catch up with you afterwards.

Without pace, your dribbling efforts will not carry much weight on the field. I've seen this countless times during my soccer career.

A player successfully dribbles his opponent but is unable to change the pace afterwards, thus resulting in the opponent clearing the ball with an aggressive tackle.

If you are a player who wants to aim higher with his dribbling skills than just dribbling your teammates during the practice sessions, then you will need to work on mastering the art of pace.

As always, a good way to improve your pace is the same as improving any new soccer skill, and that is to practice your moves on friends while having a kick around in the backyard.

While I agree that you should have fun as you train, please realize that your friends are a great opportunity to improve your dribbling skills.

So by all means enjoy practicing, but try to take it seriously at the same time. You know what it's like, it's easy to become distracted and lose focus, so be mindful of what it is you're trying to achieve.

The faster you can switch pace the more success you'll get from your dribbling attempts. It really is as simple as that!

18 HOW MANY IS ENOUGH

The question on how many opponents you should dribble past before finishing or passing the ball is not an easy one to answer.

Each situation on the field is unique and you need to decide for yourself when you should keep going or pass the ball.

This is something that comes with experience.

Quite often a player might let ego take over and think he can keep going indefinitely, dribbling by anyone and everyone who tries to stop him.

The reality is that it's easy to overdo your dribbling.

By that I mean there comes a time where losing the ball becomes inevitable.

You might think you're unstoppable, but just because you think a thing doesn't make it a reality.

Try to take on too much and yes, you will lose the ball sooner or later.

Furthermore, I can assure you that continuing to hog the ball will result in you sitting on the bench more often than not – guaranteed!

I keep my own dribbling strategy simple.

Unless circumstances dictate otherwise, I always try to keep my dribbling to a maximum of two opponents.

As soon as I get past the second, I will either attempt to finish the attack or pass the ball to better placed teammates.

After all, soccer is a team sport, not a lone show.

Remember, you are not the sole character here, needing trying to captivate an audience by showing them what a talented individual you are.

If you study professional players you will often identify this familiar pattern: as soon as he gets past one opponent he then either shoots or passes the ball.

Obviously there are times when players try to dribble two or more opponents if the conditions are right.

But even so, you will notice that after they get past the second opponent, or third at most, they usually clear the ball away, knowing that their good run will certainly expire should they hog the ball any longer.

The more skillful players you face on the pitch the more important it will be to dribble once, or twice maximum, before passing or shooting the ball.

Use your dribbling skills wisely and become an asset to your team.

Avoid being that person who just looks down at his own two feet and dribbles until his heart's content!

Being 'a part' of the team and not 'apart' from it is the only way to progress in the game of soccer.

19 PERFORMING THE MOVE TOO EARLY

Are you one of those players who are skilled at performing some amazing moves yet never able to get past an opponent on the field?

Perhaps your defenders are always able to clear the ball from you each and every time you try to pass them, leaving you bewildered and wondering how they can do it time and again!

I can almost guarantee that if you recognize yourself in the example above, then the chance is high that you are simply performing your moves too early.

By making the move "too early" I mean performing it like two yards from your opponent, and that really is too soon.

The ideal distance to execute your move is when you are about half a yard from the opponent.

Your objective is to approach close enough in order to prevent him from regaining his balance from your dribbling attempt.

This is a skill that requires a lot of practice because it needs to be timed perfectly.

The faster you are moving while performing the move, the more difficult it will be to succeed with it.

If you have carefully observed professional games on TV then you would have surely noticed how these seasoned players tend to wait for the defenders to approach them.

They simply don't want to perform the move too early.

An experienced player waits long enough to have the opponent approach them to at least a half yard or less.

In other words, the closer you are to the defender when performing your move, the more chance you have of succeeding with your dribbling attempt.

There will always be occasions where you can get around some players even if you are two or more yards away from them.

This is usually because they are too slow and too experienced.

However, the higher in the competition you play, the more talented the defenders are that you face.

Needless to say, if you want to play in competitive soccer, then it's important that you learn to perform your moves as close to the opponent as possible.

20 DEVOTE SOME TIME TO YOU BEST MOVES

OK, so let's assume you've now mastered a soccer move and are able to dribble successfully past your opponents.

You might now conclude that you simply put this new skill into your arsenal of abilities and never need practice on it again.

I mean, you can just pick it up from your dribbling wizard bag as and when you need it in order to get around an opponent, right?

Well no, I'm afraid it doesn't quite work like that.

No move will ever be mastered to the point where you never need practice it again!

Even if you are able to perform a move blindfolded, the only way to stay good at something is to maintain your skills.

This means you should regularly devote some time to practice on your dribbling talents, otherwise you will lose your edge.

Becoming complacent about one's ability is a common mistake that many players make.

Once they've learnt a skill to the level where they consider it mastered, they then stop practicing it altogether.

I say again, you need to spend time regularly working on both your weak and strong moves.

Failure to do this and you WILL lose you edge.

The question here is just how much time should you devote on practicing moves you've since mastered and those you are still poor at, and therefore need the most attention?

Well, I would spend at least one hour per week working on my strong moves as a way of maintaining what I've already become proficient at.

As for the weak moves, the time spent on grasping these would depend pretty much on how advanced they are and how fast they can be learnt.

Some players can learn a move in a single practice session, whereas others may need many sessions to learn the basics and able to perform it with any degree of dexterity.

Remember, there is a very good reason why professional soccer players practice the same dribbling moves over and over again.

You can't keep it unless you maintain it!

Make sure to adopt the same approach.

Continued practice will help you to sustain those moves you've mastered, thus keeping them as a great asset in your dribbling arsenal.

21 FOCUS ON THE SECOND TOUCH

So, you've just got past your opponent then somehow manage to get that second touch wrong.

The ball bounces several yards out of your control and over to the feet of the opposition!

I've seen this happen many times during my soccer career.

Players successfully dribble their opponents only to lose control on the ball as they touched it a second time.

It's a frustrating ordeal to say the least.

Let's consider that you are performing a step over move where you dodge to the right but then successfully switch to the left.

Now, you have successfully made the opponent move along to the right.

So far so good! But then your second touch on the ball goes horrible wrong and it bounces over to a rival player.

What's happened in the example above is that your focus has been lost because you believed the round had been won by the successful dribble.

This is where professionals separate from amateurs.

Now, if you had kept your focus you would have had a great scoring opportunity or a chance to pass the ball to a well-positioned teammate who could have finished the attack.

In order to become a dribbling wizard you will need to be self-critical, but in a positive way.

Get into the habit of studying all your mistakes constructively and then do whatever you can to correct them. Ego often plays a big role in soccer and it usually hurts, not helps, a player to develop as fast as he would like to.

I bet that many players would never admit that their second touch is simply useless. Instead, they will blame the pitch, their shoes, unfair opponents, or anything and anyone but themselves (this mindset does little to enhance one's game. A little humility, on the other hand, will help a lot!).

The faster you are going with the ball also means that it will be harder to keep it under control, thus making your second touch all the more difficult to control.

A good way to identify whether, or how much, your second touch needs to be improved on is to count the amount of successful dribbling raids you have under your belt.

The ones you failed at should be examined and analyzed constructively in order to evaluate whether your second touch needs improving. It could even turn out that there is some other technical moment that needs to be looked at which is affecting your second touch.

Remember, it is your responsibility to do this because no one can do it for you. It's fine to get feedback from others, but it will be you who ultimately has to constructively analyze your flaws and work on their solutions.

If you want to become a successful dribbling wizard then you need to start paying close attention to your second touch.

22 BEYOND THE DRIBBLING DUEL MODE

The difference between professional and amateur players is that the pros are able to see beyond the soccer move whereas amateurs rarely look past the task at hand.

As you already know, dribbling is not about demonstrating your skills to the opponents or the crowd just for the sake of showing them how good you are with the ball!

No, your primary purpose should always be to approach as close as possible to the opponent's goal and create scoring opportunities.

But, if you are just dribbling for the sake of it and to feed your own ego as a way of getting cheers from the watching crowds, then, it's time to step back as readjust your thinking into that of the "team mindset" right away.

I keep bringing this up for a reason and that is because so many promising young soccer players let their egotistical behaviors run away with themselves and ruin their chances of becoming valuable members of their team.

What this means is that there are a lot of lost opportunities when that sense of self is allowed to control an individual's mind, so please, take heed.

OK, back to the topic.

So what does it mean exactly to "see beyond the dribbling duel?"

Well, simply put it just means that you should always have a plan of action for when you get past your opponent, and that's "before" you even start challenging him.

This means you need to contemplate all your options and decide whether you should pass, shoot, or cross the ball once you've successfully got past your opponent.

Time and time again I've seen players perform amazing moves by dribbling past their opponents with precision and ease.

However, once they've passed one, two, or even three opponents in a row, they become lost as to what to do next and consequently lose the ball.

They simply did not know what to do with the ball next because they hadn't read the game properly, and that suggests they failed to think beyond the dribbling duel.

What this means is that ego had taken over, once again, and all they were concerned with was dribbling for as long as possible because they were on a role and it felt great – for them!

I must be honest here and point out that I too was one of those players once.

I got pretty good at dribbling and relished every opportunity to dribble past as many opponents as I could, when I could. I loved the rush and fed off the crowd's cheering whenever I was on a role.

But it has to be said that my team mates were not so impressed by my dribbling triumphs.

At the end of almost every one of these successful dribbling duels was a failure waiting to happen.

Why?

Because I'd have absolutely no idea what to do with the ball next!

This dithering would see me lose the ball to the opposition more often than not.

My coach would often tell me: "Mirsad? Listen to me and listen well. Once you get past your opponent you must know what to do with the ball next, otherwise, you better not dribble at all. Got it?"

Nevertheless, once you get into this way of thinking and start to actually plan ahead with each and every move, then you will become amazed of how much your performance on the pitch improves.

Like any new skill, once you've mastered it, you won't have to think about it so much.

It will become hardwired into your mindset and therefore a natural part of your play.

23 MPORTANCE OF YOUR WEAK LEG

Knowing how to dribble with one leg is great and a lot of good players are actually one-footed.

But those who get to master the dribbling art with 'both' legs will tell you that it becomes pure euphoria.

Two legged players are the true dribbling wizards out there in the world of soccer.

A player who is able to use both feet while dribbling is incredibly hard to interpret and therefore instills a lot more fear in his opponents.

For example, imagine playing on the right flank and only trusting your dominant leg for performing your dribbling skills.

Your opponent will easily predict that you will most likely go to the right in order to serve the cross.

Now, imagine that you're able to go either left or right.

Having this option will drive your opponent absolutely nuts and that in turn will give you a huge advantage over him.

Over the years I have played against few players who were great at dribbling with both feet.

To be perfectly honest, games like those usually turned out to be a real nightmare for me and my team, and therefore not the most enjoyable.

The pure frustration of never knowing quite what two-footed players planned to do next used to drive me crazy.

In fact, I'm ashamed to say that my frustration would often manifest itself into childlike tantrums, and these little outbursts sometimes saw me getting bookmarked with yellow cards.

Well, if you can't beat them, join their ranks, right?

If you can learn how to dribble with your weak leg then you really will become a great asset to your team.

Honestly, the advantage you gain over your opponents cannot be emphasized enough.

One simple strategy you can use to improve the dribbling skills with your weaker leg is to practice on all moves you are able to perform with your dominant one, using it, as the guide.

You will likely find this really hard in the beginning, and you might even think it's impossible.

However, don't give up, and definitely don't be discouraged if others laugh at your bungled attempts.

Just remember this: all the great dribbling gurus have been there and put in the hard work in order to stand out from your average players, and they stuck with it no matter what.

Also try to remember what I mentioned earlier in the book, and that is there can be no success without some failure. We learn more from our mistakes than we do our successes.

I can assure you of one thing; if you can start to train the weak leg and put it to good use, then your dribbling skills will improve beyond all former recognition.

Once you get to use both feet, then all that effort, frustration, and relentless persistence will prove to be worth every single minute.

24 IMPORTANCE OF STRENGTH

Did you know that strength plays a crucial role in your dribbling ability?

You level of strength can make or break a dribbling duel, so this is something you should regularly work on maintaining.

So what role do good strength levels actually play?

Well, being strong where it matters will allow you to use your body to shield the ball from your opponents, and also make it much harder for them to get you off balance.

One of the best examples on how strength affects dribbling skills is to study Lionel Messi and his unique style of dribbling.

If you carefully watch his dribbling attempts you will notice how he shields the ball (legally) by using his body, and also how good he is at maintain his balance in any given situation.

Notice too how he manages to slip away from his opponents when they attempt to tackle him.

Messi may not look like the Incredible Hulk, but don't let that deceive you. He possesses great strength which is one of the main reasons why he is so great at dribbling.

I would like to raise a flag of warning here though.

Knowing and controlling your strength is crucial because it's very easy to overdo this and end up with opposite results if you're not careful.

In the middle of my active soccer career one of my coaches once told me that I should spend some time in the gym working on my strength.

He said I was too skinny and that it was having a negative impact on my game.

He explained that if I simply built a little muscle where it mattered most, then I would be able to get far better results from my dribbling attempts and also improve my overall game.

Taking his advice onboard, I invested in a gym membership and started lifting weights three times a week, every week.

Sure enough, it wasn't too long before I'd built some muscle, but there was a problem. I noticed that I had also become slower because of it!

It wasn't long before I realized what the problem was.

I had been focusing far too much on the strength side of things that I had stopped working on my pace and speed with the ball.

It was this neglect which affected my performance, and not the fact that I'd become a little heavier due to the extra muscle.

While strength is an important part of your dribbling success, remember to work on it gradually and don't overdo it like I did to the point where you become obsessed.

If you do, then you run the risk of losing your pace and speed with the ball, and at the end of the day, having speed is much more important.

25 SET UP REALISTIC GOALS

Setting up "achievable" goals as you learn new dribbling skills cannot be emphasized strongly enough.

Being realistic should be a crucial part of your overall strategy to develop your skills.

I'm a firm believer in taking notes.

By writing your dribbling goals down before each practice session, and then evaluating them afterwards, is a simple yet effect approach.

You simply look at the things you were able to achieve and those which still need more work.

One of the biggest mistakes I made when trying to learn new dribbling moves was to set up highly unrealistic goals for myself.

In my naivety, I thought that just because someone else was able to learn a specific move in a single day, then I was going to be able to do the same.

However, if by the end of the day I had failed to master a new move, I'd become frustrated and disappointed with myself.

In other words, I would beat myself up.

I know now that putting oneself down serves no useful purpose whatsoever.

So whatever you do, please don't make the same mistakes that I did.

It is really important for you to understand that comparing your skills with others has no benefits at all, especially when comparing yourself in a negative light.

If one of your friends or teammates is able to learn a new move in no time at all, that doesn't mean he's necessarily a better player, it just means he was able to learn something quicker, that's all!

I can remember once how one of my best friends was truly amazing at performing all kinds of moves, and also quick to pick up on any new ones.

If I'm honest, looking back now, I was probably a bit jealous of him if the truth be known.

However, I was always one of the starting eleven and he usually began every game on the bench, despite the fact that he was a dribbling genius when compared to me.

What I'm trying to say is that despite my friend's ability to learn moves faster than me, I was still a better overall player.

There is no time frame for how fast you should learn a specific move.

All you need to do is stay focused, be positive, and stick with it to the point where you can use it successfully to dribble your opponents in a competition.

In fact, it's been my experience that the longer it takes to master a new move, the better you become at it.

Again, please, whatever you do, don't make the same mistake as I did and become impatient and envious of others.

If you do, it will only serve to decrease your confidence on the pitch.

If your confidence takes a nosedive, then it will set you back at a time where you're trying to progress forward with your game.

In other words, you'll end up with the reverse of what you're trying to achieve.

Make sure to always set up realistic goals and be good to yourself. Patience and persistence always prevails in the end.

Gradually work on your skills and refuse to get disappointed if progress is slower than you anticipated.

26 TRACK THE PROGRESS

This is something I used to believe was quite unnecessary, that was until I implemented it into my own development program.

The day I started tracking my own dribbling skills was the day I realized it was something I should have done much, much sooner!

It is really important to objectively analyze both your dribbling performance and progress in order to get the most out most of this strategy.

You should start by reflecting over you strong points. These might be good step overs, strong pace, etc., and then look at the areas where you are less good.

That might be poor strength or loss of focus after passing your opponent, as two examples.

After every game you should evaluate where you lacked in something and then write down what you plan to do in order to improve in these areas.

Come the next match, you then put your improved plan into action and reflect on how well it worked, or didn't work, as the case may be.

This is something I used to do after each of my games and I quickly discovered several mistakes I was making while practicing on my moves.

I picked up on how these mistakes were negatively affecting my dribbling attempts during the games.

One of the things I spotted by tracking my progress was how I tended to perform the moves too early instead of waiting for the opponent to get closer (ideally this should be at least a half yard).

Another thing I found out was the importance of changing pace.

By improving in this area, I was able to have my opponents losing their balance.

After identifying and working on improving my mistakes, it was only the fastest of the fast opponents who could actually catch me up once I got by them.

Improving these two mistakes did wonders for my dribbling duels once I'd perfected them. I came to realize that if I kept monitoring my dribbling progress – at all times – I would always be a step ahead of my game.

Being able to identify any new pitfalls, or the return of bad habits, is an invaluable tool to have at your disposal.

Even if you are really skilled at dribbling, there will always be things that you can do to improve still further.

Remember, as human beings we can never stop improving, adapting, learning new things, or other more economical ways to perform the same or similar tasks.

A smart player will constantly take an objective look at his abilities and seek new ways on how to improve his skill set.

This is why I recommend this strategy to you, especially if you are serious about your game and want to move your soccer career up to the next level.

Reaching higher goals is certainly a lot more work and dedication than just settling to be an average player, but the rewards for all that effort can be immense.

27 WATCH PROFESSIONAL GAMES

Most of my dribbling skills were inspired by carefully watching professional players on TV and then trying to copy their moves.

Closely analyzing a player's moves is completely different to just watching the game.

It's crucial that you focus on scrutinizing their dribbling skills, and avoid getting emotionally involved in the match at all costs.

When you get emotionally wrapped up in an actual match, then your analysis will carry far less weight.

If you are to pick up on the details of individual players, then stay totally focused at all times.

I always used to keep a notebook by my side while watching professional games on TV.

By jotting down key points for each move as it happened proved to be incredibly useful to my own self-improvement.

Telling yourself: "Oh, I will make a note of that later," Just doesn't work.

You will be surprised at how quickly these things slip the mind, which is why writing them down as they occur is really the only way to go with this.

Why this strategy worked so well with me and continues to work well with many others, is because it's a proven way to learn things much faster.

This method allows you to focus on the important things without wasting time on those things which are less important or totally insignificant.

I recommend you watch at least two professional games on TV each week.

Get into the habit of analyzing the moves performed by individual players, and then write down the key points as you pick up on them.

Make sure you don't just focus on the fancy looking moves either.

Analyze the more traditional ones like the fake kick, and step over, etc.

These are the fundamentals of your dribbling arsenal.

You may also record the games if you have a media player that can handle that.

You then get to analyze the players afterwards, frame by frame if you want to, until you fully understand the key points and how to perform a particular move.

I have a whole collection of old tapes from when Ronaldo Luís Nazário de Lima was the undisputed number one dribbling wizard in the world, and I wouldn't get rid of them for all the tea in China.

I can say with complete honestly that I would never have learned to perform step overs properly, using both feet, without studying Ronaldo's dribbling skills on tape.

Being told how to perform a move is one thing, but seeing it repeatedly by learning from visual recordings, and in your own time, is by far the most productive approach.

I learned other dribbling moves as well using this method, but the step overs become the fundament of my dribbling arsenal.

In retrospect, step overs have helped me get past a great many defenders during my soccer days.

So please, make sure you utilize this strategy and really focus on getting the most out of it.

Study seriously, and practice religiously, and you will soon get to see the true benefits of learning directly from the pros.

28 ASK YOUR FRIENDS TO EVALUATE YOUR MOVES

If you have not thought about this strategy, or are a little put off by it, then don't be!

I can say with hand on heart that it works very well.

I have found that those friends who are also keen on soccer are only too happy to help out.

But you must insist that they are totally honest, albeit in a constructive way, and void of all teasing.

As you kick the ball around in the backyard ask your friends what they think about your dribbling skills.

Also ask them what, if anything, they believe you could improve upon.

You may be amazed at just how many valuable tips you get from your buddies, and how much these snippets of constructive feedback can improve your overall dribbling performance.

One of my best friends, who I had been playing soccer with for several years in the same team, always used to evaluate my dribbling skills and told me in all honesty what he believed I could improve upon.

He was playing as the right fullback while my position was right midfielder.

Needless to say this worked very well as we played close to each other and could therefore monitor each other's moves on the field.

We often noticed that we found similar areas in each other's dribbling that could use a little re-tweaking.

This helped us to identify more easily what we should place more emphasis upon.

Now don't get me wrong, negative criticism, even when said in a constructive manner, can sometimes be hard to take, especially if you've just played a bad game.

But you can't ask for honest advice and then get upset if you're told something you'd sooner not hear.

When you invite feedback - in all its forms - you really do have to wear your rhinoceros skin and take stuff on the chin.

More importantly is that you must listen to what's being said otherwise this strategy is fruitless.

The good thing about getting a friend to monitor your dribbling is that you get to practice together in the backyard.

My friend would act like a real opponent as I practiced on my weaknesses and vice versa.

The most important thing about the "buddy method" is that you have to make a pact with each other and promise to always tell the truth with no holds barred.

Holding back on something, or winding each other up for the sake of a giggle, will do nothing to improve your dribbling skills, so this has to be taken seriously.

29 USING A SMALLER BALL

The first time I saw someone using a small ball for practicing dribbling skills was on a video documentary about Diego Armando Maradona.

He was using a ball about the same size of those ones used in handball.

He was performing some amazing dribbling moves with it too.

I found this really fascinating and wondered whether I should try using a small ball when working on my own dribbling skills as well, so decided to give it a try.

I borrowed a handball from one of my friends and began to practice on my dribbling without having any real expectations from it.

I wanted to learn the snake move first, also called the Elastico.

This is where you push the ball with the outside of your foot (while still slightly touching it), and then bring the same foot around.

The trick here is to quickly pull the ball in the opposite direction which is useful for when your opponent is trying to tackle.

I managed to get it right few times with the small ball, but I also slipped several times as it was raining outside.

Therefore, I suggest not practicing with the small ball on a wet and slippery surface.

Anyway, after practicing with this small ball for few days I was keen to try my newfound skills out with a regular sized soccer ball.

To my surprise the moves felt much easier to perform, and I mean "much" easier.

It's a bit like coming off a full-sized snooker table and onto a pool table.

If you've ever done this you will just know how easy it becomes to pot the ball when everything appears bigger and closer.

So I continued practicing on my moves with the small ball and those same moves just keep getting better and better when playing with the regular sized ball.

I demonstrated the moves to my teammates during a practice session.

There were genuinely amazed, and asked what I had had done that allowed me to improve my dribbling skills so much in such a short space of time?

As I didn't wanted to reveal my secret, I just told them I had spent a lot of time working hard on my dribbling and this was simply the result of my commitment.

The moves worked great during the games as well.

My dribbling performance was so much more successful compared to how it was before I discovered the small ball as a tool for practicing.

So, if you have not tried practicing your moves with a small ball, I suggest you give this method a go.

If you can work with it, then you too will get some great results.

30 SURPRISING MOMENT

The ability to surprise your opponent and do the unexpected is what separates the true dribbling masters from your Joe Average players.

If you're anything like me and watch professional games really closely, then I bet you know the kind of players I'm talking about.

These guys are able to perform moves you would never have a thought of.

This is one of the reasons why these players have become professional.

Being able to constantly surprise and perform unexpected moves is a gift that works extremely well in sport.

Learning this skill is not like practicing on your shooting or heading as it requires you play in a competition against real opponents.

It can be hard to explain surprise moves, but I will give you an example on something that I consider being both surprising and unexpected.

This is one of my favorite moves.

The idea is to pretend to receive the ball with my right foot but in reality tapping it very slightly with the outside of the foot and having it go past my opponent.

I would then quickly change pace and sprint off in the opposite direction where, hopefully, the ball is already there waiting for me.

While this is a pretty simple move it works really well when performed correctly.

Unless you are a very slow player, you will have given yourself an advantage of several yards if you get this right.

A move like this is a clear example of a surprising and unexpected dribble.

The more chances you get to work on this, the more opportunities you will have to improve your dribbling skills.

Remember that all the best dribbling masters are able to perform moves that no one actually anticipates.

It goes without saying that a talent like this gives them a huge advantage on the field.

Obviously the true dribbling masters also possess all the other necessary skills too, like pace, ball control and so on, but having the added ability to produce unexpected moves at the drop of a hat is what makes them stand out from the rest.

If your ambition is to become one of these A-list players, then you need to pay attention to this skill and start to work it into your game.

31 ANTICIPATE LIKE THE PROS

Being able to anticipate a situation is yet another skill which separates amateurs from professionals.

A real pro will always know which move to perform before the ball even reaches his feet, whereas amateurs rarely think that far ahead.

Learning how to anticipate is essential if you are to become good.

It is something that should develop into an integral part of your overall game.

When you don't perform as well as you had hoped to during a match, on reflection, you will often see that it was because you had failed read a situation and plan your next move in advance.

I'm sure you have seen a lot of amateur players receive the ball and then just stand there without really knowing quite what move to perform next.

This is a clear example of failing to anticipate.

Remember, in order to take your dribbling skills up a level, you are going to have to learn how to think one step ahead.

The higher up in the competition you get to play, the more important it becomes to anticipate and plan your moves in advance.

I personally didn't become aware of how key this skill was until I started to face opponents from the highest division here in Sweden.

In one of the games I was playing against a Swedish national team fullback called Alexander Östlundh.

All you need to know about him is that he was really good.

As the game progressed, I realized that I had been losing focus and failed to anticipate.

The consequence of that meant I hadn't even been able to get past Alexander Östlundh; not even once!

With an adjustment to mindset, I reset my focus.

The next time I was about to receive the ball, I decided to try a simple turn feint.

What I did was to pretended I was about to turn left but instead shot off to the right.

I heard him approaching from the rear as the ball rolled towards me.

Then, just as the ball arrived at my feet, I successfully performed the move.

This is one of my greatest dribbling memories of all time. It demonstrated how my moves can work really well, even on professional players.

It was indeed a great feeling.

As I mentioned earlier, learning how to anticipate is what will separate you from the amateurs.

If you want to become a successful player and achieve great success with your dribbling skills, then you will have to incorporate anticipation and forward planning into your game.

32 DISCOVERING YOUR OWN DRIBBLING STYLE

If you are like me and all the other soccer enthusiasts out there, then I'm sure you have your own favorite player, someone who, in your opinion, you consider to be the ultimate dribbling guru.

While it is great to emulate your favorite player and attempt to copy all of his moves, you will need to work on developing your very own dribbling style.

It's been my experience that a lot of budding soccer players tend to think that dribbling is all about performing fancy moves and entertaining the crowd.

They believe that if the crowd isn't impressed, then the move is most likely lacking in glory.

Failing to entertain the spectators can lead them to perform moves that are perhaps enjoyable to watch, yet completely useless for the game as a whole.

I used to spend countless of hours trying to copy my favorite player, the great Ronaldo Luís Nazário de Lima.

One summer, the only skills I practiced on were the ones Ronaldo performed.

Despite my best efforts, and to my great disappointment, I still could not even get close to dribbling like him.

Acceptance can be a great asset though. Admitting defeat at my attempts to mimic Ronaldo Luís Nazário de Lima, I then decided to try another approach.

I chose to work on developing my own dribbling style, and it turned out to be a very good move, and I have never regretted it.

Although I have never been able to perform the super fancy moves that Ronaldo performed to drive his challenger's nuts, I am still able to get past my opponents with simple, yet highly efficient moves of my own making.

This is why I recommend you work at developing your own style of dribbling, and avoid trying to copy that of your favorite player.

Just look at all other great dribbling wizards like Messi and Cristiano Ronaldo to see what I mean.

Each one of them has developed their own unique style. There is no question of doubt that their individual techniques are what bolstered their careers.

Just remember that you are you, and not a clone of somebody else.

Find your own form and develop it, as it is you and your talent that will shine through in the end.

33 GET THAT BALL BACK

I have lost count how many times I've seen players trying to dribble their opponents, losing the ball, and then standing there as they wait for the next opportunity to present itself.

This is an approach that will do absolutely nothing to turn you into a successful dribbling wiz.

A true dribbling master continues to work hard even when he loses the ball to an opponent.

There have been many times where I've tried to dribble my opponent, lost the ball, regained possession immediately afterwards, and then successfully got past him.

The point I'm making is this: just because you lose the ball that doesn't have to mean your dribbling attempt is over.

Providing your opponent doesn't pass the ball on, then you still have a good opportunity to get it back and challenge him a second time.

The worst thing you can do is to just stand there looking bewildered, pretending perhaps that it is someone else's fault why you lost the ball.

Having a defeatist mindset does not only negatively impact a player's performance. An idle player also has a knock-on effect by irritating the team too, and we all know what happens to a team when moral is affected.

I've seen plenty of potentially great dribbling stars in the making who were cursed with this attitude. Sadly, guys like these never get to reach professional soccer. Lost opportunities caused by a player's inability to challenge defeat, is such a waste of what would otherwise be raw talent.

You don't want to be one of those defeatist players because you will only waste your forte. When it comes to team soccer, there are a number of boxes to tick, and failure to tick enough of the right boxes can result in your downfall.

Not chasing the ball after losing it is one of the biggest mistakes players make. They get it into their heads that dribbling is just about performing moves, and anything outside of that will be taken care of by the other team members.

If anyone reading here doubts what I'm saying, then please watch a professional game on TV. It won't be too long before you get to see how often players try to regain the ball after losing it to a dribbling duel.

You can be pretty sure that they will go after the opponent and do everything in their power to recover possession of the ball.

You can be the ultimate dribbling wiz, but if you fail to utilize this skill and follow through after losing the ball, then your dribbling attempts will not be worth much at a team level.

If you can identify with this flaw then it's time to change your behavior, and fast! Players who just stand around, waiting for teammates to do the grunt work, and pass the ball to them, will find that they spend a lot more time on the bench than on the pitch.

34 RIGHT MOVES AT RIGHT TIME

Using the right move for the right situation can mean the difference between a great dribbling showdown and total failure.

There might be a number of moves that can be performed for a given situation, but you always need to evaluate how effective a particular move actually is for what you aim to achieve.

For example, using a fake kick is ideal for creating a shooting opportunity outside the opponent's 18 yard box. However, that same move is not so effectual more centrally on the field.

Another example is the use of the step over.

This is just great for getting past your opponents at the flank, but it can be far less effective if you want to quickly create a shooting opportunity outside the 18 yard box.

As you can see, learning how to determine the best move for a particular situation is a skill that requires you to analyze each situation carefully, but quickly, and then go with the one your gut believes will work out the best.

No one can give you a blueprint for this. There is no simple answer as all situations are totally unique.

It is experience and skill that will determine how good you become at predicting the best move at any given time.

I mean, you need to fail somewhat in order to succeed with this.

Remember what I said earlier in the book about how there can be no success in soccer without some failure?

And also how we learn more from our botched attempts than we do our accomplishments?

What works, what doesn't work, and the best way to play a situation, is something that comes with experience and mindfulness.

They only surefire way to develop here is to play in real competitions as often as you can.

As with all other skills, there will come a time where this will become a natural part of your game, and you will intuitively know what move best suits the situation in hand.

Like most other young players who were working on their game, I also had problems learning this skill in the beginning.

It was not uncommon for me to perform the wrong moves in a given situation, but this was only down to my lack of experience at the time.

It was only by making wrong decisions though, that I got to learn how to later make better informed moves.

You will find this too. As you become more experienced this skill will develop naturally within you. Before you know it, you will instinctively know what move to use for a specific situation.

If you don't see improvements happening as quickly as you would like, then please don't get disheartened.

It actually took me two seasons to develop this ability, and it might take you some time too. Just know that so long as you stick with it, then you WILL become better.

I often say in my books that patience and persistence will prevail in the end, and that is because this is so true. So be patient, stay persistent, and watch yourself grow.

35 BODY FEINTS

When you are approaching your opponent for a dribbling duel you should never be completely rigid.

Instead, try to perform small body shakes, or bobs, as a way to confuse them.

If you study professional soccer players you will notice how they carry out all manner of body movements, and also how they sway their heads around quite a bit.

There's a very good reason for all of this.

Professionals do this 'thing' with the body because they know it's off-putting to their opponents.

Ducking and dodging is a great way to confuse a challenger. Master these body feints and it will contribute greatly towards the success of your dribbling duels.

There is no specific template for how many times you should feint with your body or what kind of movements you should perform.

This is one thing that has to be natural to you, and not something you consciously contemplate as you confront an opponent.

The idea here is to find your own style when feinting with the body.

All you need to do is test things out as a way of perfecting your own moves.

Backyard soccer is a great place for experimenting.

For my own style, I like to move a few times to the right and also use my hip to give the impression that I will go off in a specific direction.

But like I said, this is an individual thing and you need to work with the natural rhythm of your own body. Do this, and you should be able to come up with something that works for you, your build and your body type.

A good place to start would be to study the body feints of professional players, especially the Brazilian ones, as they tend to have a natural talent for this skill.

Don't be shy to try out a few ideas that you pick up from the professionals.

Any given move might seem unnatural and awkward to you personally, whereas another might fit you like a glove.

Just have fun and try out a variety of body feints, and you will surely find something that feels right and works a treat.

As with all new skills, avoid trying to mimic others like for like.

Take some ideas and make them your own by developing them into your own style of play.

It took me several months to invent my own style of body feints, and a bit longer still before I became totally comfortable using them during the games.

But I got there in the end, and they have served me very well ever since.

Remember this; there are still a lot of players out there who don't realize the true importance of body feints, but now that you do, this gives you yet another advantage on the soccer field.

36 BALANCE FOOT

There's a good chance you've never reflected over this, but did you know that your balancing foot plays a big role in whether your dribbling attempts will be a success or a total failure?

Your balancing foot contributes to the success of your dribbling in three ways:
1. Improved balance
2. Ability to change direction quickly
3. Ability to shield the ball better.

I'm sure you've seen players that are completely dependent upon on one foot, yet some of them can be as good at dribbling as many of the two-footed players.

The reason is because they are really good at taking advantage of their balancing foot during dribbling attempts.

A perfect example of this is Diego Armando Maradona, who was totally one-footed, yet still considered by many to be the best soccer player ever.

In my opinion, he is the best example on how to take advantage of your balancing foot during dribbling attempts.

Throughout the early years of my soccer career, I never actually paid much attention to my balancing foot.

In fact, it would feel completely weird whenever I tried to handle the ball with it.

However, a coach once told me that even if I don't use my balancing foot to handle the ball (this would change later in my career), I should still pay attention to how I can use it more effectively.

He said that the position and direction of this foot will play an important role in the outcome of my dribbling duels.

He explained that it helps to control the speed of the ball and also helps to change pace easier.

As I started to pay close attention to what he said, I noticed that I was able to coordinate my balancing foot with the other one.

This new skill saw an improvement in my dribbling too.

The valuable lesson to be learned here is that although you can still achieve some good average dribbling skills without paying attention to your balancing foot, by 'paying attention' to it, you become even more proficient.

37 DROPPING THE SHOULDER

This is one dribbling skill that is really easy to learn, but can do absolute wonders for your game.

When done properly, it can help you get you past any opponent, no matter how skillful he might be.

The idea is to approach your opponent at high speed and then feint in one direction by dropping your shoulder, and go the other way at the last minute.

In order to succeed with it you will need to lean your shoulder slightly down and then quickly change pace as you shoot off in the other direction.

It's also worth noting that this works better when you involve your leg a bit too.

If you slightly bend the leg in the same direction it will make this move look all the more convincing.

This is a simple yet very effective skill to learn.

It has certainly helped me get past countless defenders while playing at the flank, but it can be used successfully on whichever position you are playing.

As with most of these dribbling skills, its success depends pretty much on how well you are able to convince the opponent.

If he genuinely believes you are going to go in the direction you are suggesting, then you've cracked it.

If you are left footed, then you would fake by using your left shoulder.

As the opponent moves over to that direction, you then quickly move the ball to the right foot and sprint off rightwards.

One of the best examples of a professional player who is able to utilize this skill with great success is Thierry Henry (French striker for New York Red Bulls).

Quiet often when he approaches an opponent at high speed, Henry drops his shoulder and thus creates a great scoring opportunity.

I know from experience that so many players still believe that dribbling should be as fancy as possible, providing both entertainment and success, but the reality is that this only tends to complicate things unnecessarily.

While I agree that dropping the shoulder isn't the most impressive of moves, it is still really effective for getting past your opponent.

Always bear in mind that dribbling is all about getting results, and to do that you need to get passed those who try to stop you.

How you do this is not the issues here, it's whether you succeed or not that's important.

38 WAIT FOR THE OPPONENT

One of my best kept secrets for getting past opponents with a minimum of effort is to wait for him to go for the ball.

Although it might not look fancy, I can guarantee you this: it will be one of the best dribbling skills in your arsenal if you put in the time and effort to learn it properly.

The secret of this skill is to have the opponent believe he can clear the ball away with relative ease.

Then, just as he goes for it, you take the ball away and get past him.

As you can see, there is a bit of a mind game involved here, but then soccer as a whole is pretty much a mental challenge as well as a physical one.

In my experience, this skill is especially effective on less competent opponents as they tend to attack the ball as the moment you approach them.

Opponents at higher level competition are more knowledgeable, and know that a single mistake on their side will allow you to pass them.

Therefore, they are less likely to go for the ball too soon.

Waiting for the opponent to go for the ball first is really effective when you are playing at the flank.

Here, a challenger will either attempt to slide tackle you or aggressively attack the ball.

The main risk with this confidence trick is that an opponent can easily clear the ball if you are not fast enough on your feet.

The key is to wait as long as possible before you pull the ball away.

The longer you can hold back, the more chance there is of the challenger losing his balance.

Once he loses his balance he's lost the duel.

You are now able to just pull the ball away and leave him behind, feeling both beaten and bewildered.

Remember, dribbling doesn't always have to look fancy.

Be mindful of that fact that during any dribbling duel, your one and only task is to get around the opponent first and foremost.

How you get by him, and what skills you use, is not so relevant.

Your objective is to use any legal move in you dribbling arsenal to achieve results.

39 IGNORING PROVOKING OPPONENTS

The most irritating part of dribbling is when you have an opponent mocking you all the time during the duel, uttering things about how useless you are.

I've faced several players over the years who make all kinds of noises, and say whatever they feel like, just try to make you lose your focus during the game.

If you are new to the game of soccer this could seriously affect your dribbling attempts.

Unless you are naturally blessed with an incredibly thick skin, then you will likely move your focus from dribbling to reacting on the scornful remarks of the challenger.

The best thing you can do with opponents like this is to simply ignore them and let you dribbling skills speak for themselves. Easier said than done though, I know, but ignore them you must! You will have to develop a thicker skin when on the pitch.

If you don't, then the way taunts negatively affect your game will become your known weakness in soccer circles.

Once a challenger realizes he can't actually make you lose focus by his hecklings, he will soon get bored and stop bothering you.

I know this because I have been in this situation myself in the past. Opponents would talk nonstop about how poor my skills were as they marked me.

They would say things like I was so useless that I should quit soccer altogether, and other such hurtful remarks.

In the beginning of my career I reacted negatively to these provocations, and even got myself a red card once because of an inability to control my temper.

However, I soon learned that by reacting as I did I was giving these bullies exactly what they wanted. The day came where I wasn't prepared to give in to them anymore, ever!

Once I learned to ignore these opponents, I could see how my newfound poise would turn their snide remarks against them.

By totally ignoring their attempts to intimidate me, it was they who ended up getting irritated and losing focus.

If you are already someone who is able to ignore bullyboy players, then you are in a pole position.

If, however, you are like I was, then you will need to practice a bit of self-control and learn how to switch off to their taunting.

It can be done, even though it might take a bit of practice, but adjusting your mindset is very doable with a little effort.

There are also studies which show that soccer players who react negatively to provoking opponents will generally decrease their performance by 50%.

Just think what you could achieve by learning to ignore all kinds of irritating jibes on the field, and focus solely on dribbling your opponents.

I will end this chapter with a very apt and wise quote from a Dr. Wayne Dyer (an American self-help author and motivational speaker). He said:

"If you change the way you look at things, the things you look at change."

40 GET INSPIRED BY YOUR TEAMMATES

One of my best tips for accelerating the learning curve of new moves, and increasing dribbling skills in general, is to get inspired by teammates.

Being inspired naturally instills inspiration.

Watch what types of moves other team players perform during the practice sessions and games, and then try to learn from them.

I would never have become quite as good at the step over move as I did if it wasn't for one of my teammates.

Getting to watch him perform close up was invaluable.

He pointed out one or two things I needed to correct in order to dribble my opponents more successfully during games.

He also appreciated that I asked him for help.

This was proof to him that he was doing something right during the games and was helping his team.

Again, a good team effort is all about teamwork, and this applies off the pitch as well as on it.

This "helping each other out" is a win-win situation as your teammate will be inspired by you seeking his advice.

And you are already enthused by his skills, yet become even more encouraged when he offers to help you improve your own game.

I need to raise a word of warning here though.

Not all team members will be so quick to take time out to help another.

In every team, there will be some who are just too arrogant, too selfish, and too paranoid to care.

Some guys simply don't want to share their tips and secrets with their fellow players because they are afraid that by helping others to improve might result in them losing their own place on the team.

Personally, I think such paranoia is unjust.

I believe that in order to keep something you have to give it away, i.e. by helping you, you are indirectly helping me, and vice versa.

So, if you do get knocked back by seeking the help of someone whose play inspires you, don't let it get to you.

Just understand that every team has its lone players and that it's nothing personal, it's simply the way they are.

Just move on and forget about them and find someone who is more accommodating.

By the way, don't make the mistake of not asking someone because you think they are too busy or too talented to give you the time of day.

It's been my experience that most team players are only too happy to help another, and if you don't ask, you will never know.

41 IMPROVING YOUR HOP

The hop is simply the up and down movement of your supporting foot during a dribbling duel.

The more you can coordinate this movement naturally into your style, the better your dribbling results will be.

You might be thinking that this is a tiny part of your overall dribbling technique, and in some ways it is, but you should still remember that it is a highly important one.

If you study Messi, and other dribbling wizards, you will notice how their supporting foot is always moving and up and down slightly with a natural motion.

Of course, this is not the only reason for their exceptional dribbling skills, but it is an important and significant part of the overall dribbling technique nonetheless, which is why it needs attention.

Even though this skill will be improved indirectly it every time you drive the ball forward, you do still need to put some extra work into it.

What I used to do was put ten cones in a zigzag formation and then approach each of them at high speed while trying to take as many hops as possible.

In the beginning I didn't notice any significant improvements in my dribbling.

However, after a few months of practicing, things started to get noticeably better.

What also surprised me was how I felt more comfortable with the ball as I approached my opponents for a dribbling duel.

I know that this can be a really boring skill to work on, but it has to be done so best not to think too much and just get on with it.

Try to stay focused and be mindful of the fact that it will boost your overall dribbling technique, and any improvement will have a positive impact on your overall ability to get past your opponents.

Remember, if you want to reach the stars and become a dribbling wizard, then you'll need to work on the boring parts as well as those things which are more enjoyable.

42 VISUALIZING YOUR MOVES

The advantage of visualizing moves is something I discovered while listening to an interview with one of the best dribbling stars of all time, and that is Mr. Ronaldo Luís Nazário de Lima.

He pointed out that each player should try to visualize his moves as often as possible.

Why?

Well, visualization helps a player to perform his moves with greater success.

This is a tried and tested formula that works.

I must admit that I had hard believing in this in the beginning. I just could not see how visualizing a soccer move would help me perform it better in real life.

Despite my skepticism, when the great Ronaldo Luís Nazário de Lima speaks, it would be a foolish player to ignore him, so I had to at least give this a go.

You know what I'm about to say next, right?

To my surprise, after visualizing my soccer moves over the course of several days, I noticed a marked improvement in my dribbling skills.

Needless to say I decided to incorporate visualization into my overall soccer training program.

This is something that can be done at anytime, anywhere. I used to spend one hour each day visualizing my moves on the school bus.

As soon as I learned a new move I added it to my visualizing bank.

By now, I had quite a collection of them in my dribbling arsenal, many of which I could bring to the forefront of my mind during games.

I also went back to older games where I visualized performing the moves better during those situations where I failed to get past opponents.

Thinking about past bungles, and then visualizing them in a successful light, really helped me avoid making the same mistakes again.

Furthermore, visualization also helped me to become a smarter player by picking the right moves for right situations.

If you're still not convinced that visualizing could improve your dribbling skills, all I will say is don't mock it until you've at least given it a go.

You have nothing to lose by trying, and it's also a great way to constructively utilize time that would otherwise be wasted, such as travelling on the school bus, standing in a queue, or listening to music, as three examples.

You might also want to try visualizing your moves as you prepare for a game, as this is the time when you will be most focused.

Remember, visualizing could do wonders for your dribbling skills, as it did with mine, and prevent you from making the same mistakes over and over again.

So please, listen to my advice here and make sure you give it a chance.

If you don't, then you could be missing out on a real gem of a trick here!

43 SHIELDING THE BALL

As you dribble the ball, there will usually be opponents approaching alongside you trying to clear it away.

The easiest way to keep the ball away from an attacking opponent is to have it on the opposite side.

For example, if you are playing at the flank and the opponent is approaching from the left, then you would simply move the ball to the right side.

This will help you to shield the ball easier with your body, thus making it harder for the opponent to clear it away.

A lot of players make the mistake of slowing down and waiting for the opponent to attack as they attempt to shield the ball.

Instead of doing this, a much better approach is to drive the ball forward, even if you are forced to do it with your less powerful foot.

Even if you can't get past the opponent, you can still gain valuable yards by driving the ball forward while shielding it.

I have known several players over the years that based their whole dribbling strategy on this very technique, and with great success.

Some of these guys were not that fast which often meant they would have their opponent catch them up on the side and attack the ball.

However, they would use their body really effectively to shield the ball as they kept it moving forwards.

It wasn't that unusual for an attacking opponent to become so frustrated at his failed attempts to gain control of the ball that the situation would end in a foul.

This would obviously result in a free kick near to the opponent's 18 yard box, from where there was a great opportunity to score.

As you see, being able to successfully shield the ball is another important part of your dribbling technique.

The sooner you start using it, the more success you will have on the field.

44 TOUCHES ON THE BALL

Touching, or tapping, the ball as many times as possible as you approach your opponent is another important aspect of dribbling.

Mastering soft touches on the ball, combined with speed, will help you enormously when it comes to getting past your opponents.

In fact, even a player without any other real dribbling skills could still perform pretty well if he manages to use this technique effectively.

While you will improve your dribbling with this method, it is also worth mentioning that your overall ball control will also improve as an indirect result of learning this skill.

All the great dribbling wizards will perform countless touches on the ball as they dribble, which goes to prove just how important this actually is.

You can easily work on improving this skill by becoming mindful about it.

Just remember to touch the ball as many times as possible during your backyard playing, team practices, and competition.

Before you know it, this will be one more talent that you will be performing subconsciously.

Like all new skills, some of you will pick this up in no time at all, whereas others might take a little longer, but you will all get better at it with practice.

The point is to keep trying.

The only failure a player can make is the failure to try, and remember, it is patience and persistence that prevails in the end.

I can personally assure you of one thing, and that is it will all be worth it in the end.

I have seen time and time again, player after player – including me - those who practiced, without complaint, got to see their dribbling skills improve by several levels.

In general, the longer you have been playing without using this technique, the longer it will take to incorporate it into your style of dribbling, but don't let that put you off.

It's frequently the case where those who take more time to master a new skill, often become better at it than those who picked it up almost instantly.

ENDING...

My last advice to you is following: If you have a dream, then do not give it up just because someone says that you will not make it and remember to always believe in yourself no matter what!